C000161771

EXPLORE J

Travel Guide

The Citi-scaper

Table of Contents

Introduction

Jordan is a land of ancient civilizations, captivating landscapes, and vibrant cultures. Located in the heart of the Middle East, Jordan is a small country that packs a big punch. From the desert landscapes of Wadi Rum to the archaeological wonders of Petra, Jordan offers visitors a wealth of experiences and adventures.

For first-time visitors, Jordan can be a bit overwhelming. With so much to see and do, it can be hard to know where to start. That's where a travel guide to Jordan comes in. This guide will provide you with all the information you need to plan your trip to Jordan, from visas and vaccinations to the best places to stay and eat.

One of the highlights of any trip to Jordan is a visit to Petra, the ancient city carved into the rock face. This UNESCO World Heritage Site is one of the most impressive archaeological sites in the world, and it's a must-see for any visitor to Jordan. But there's much more to see in Jordan than just Petra. From the Roman ruins at Jerash to the

Crusader castles of Ajloun and Karak, history buffs will have plenty to keep them busy.

Jordan is also home to some of the most stunning natural landscapes in the world. The Wadi Rum desert, with its towering red sandstone cliffs, is a favorite among adventure travelers. You can take a jeep tour through the desert, go rock climbing, or even spend the night in a Bedouin camp.

For those who prefer a more relaxing vacation, Jordan has plenty to offer as well. The Dead Sea, located at the lowest point on earth, is a unique and unforgettable experience. You can float effortlessly in the salty waters and enjoy the healing properties of the mineral-rich mud.

Of course, no trip to Jordan would be complete without sampling the delicious local cuisine. From falafel and hummus to shawarma and mansaf, Jordanian food is flavorful and varied.

In this travel guide to Jordan, we'll cover everything you need to know to plan the perfect trip. We'll discuss the best time to visit, how to get around, what to see and do, and where to stay and eat.

Chapter 1

Overview

Jordan, popularly referred to as the Hashemite Kingdom of Jordan, is a sovereign country located in the heart of the Middle East. Bordered by Saudi Arabia to the south and east, Iraq to the northeast, Syria to the north, and Israel and Palestine to the west, Jordan is situated in a highly strategic location. With a history spanning thousands of years, Jordan boasts a rich cultural heritage and diverse landscapes that have captured the imagination of travelers from around the world.

Among the many tourist destinations in Jordan, the ancient city of Petra stands out as a must-visit site. The city, which was carved into rock over 2,000 years ago by the Nabataeans, is a UNESCO World Heritage Site and a wonder of the ancient world. Often called the "Rose City" due to the color of the rock, Petra is a magnificent showcase of ancient architecture and engineering.

Visitors can explore the numerous temples, tombs, and other structures, including the famous Treasury and Monastery, which continue to amaze and inspire visitors to this day.

Another must-see attraction in Jordan is the Dead Sea, which is the lowest point on Earth and is known for its high salt content and therapeutic mud. Visitors can float in the Dead Sea and enjoy the unique experience of weightlessness while also taking in the stunning views of the surrounding mountains.

Jordan is also home to numerous other historical and cultural sites, including the Roman ruins of Jerash, the Umayyad desert castle of Quseir Amra, and the Crusader castle of Karak. The capital city of Amman is also worth exploring, with its mix of modern and traditional architecture, bustling markets, and excellent restaurants.

For outdoor enthusiasts, Jordan offers a wide range of activities, including hiking, camping, and rock climbing in the Wadi Rum desert, exploring the Dana Biosphere Reserve, and trekking through the canyons of the Mujib Nature Reserve.

Jordan is also known for its warm and welcoming people, who are eager to share their culture and traditions with visitors. Whether it's enjoying a cup of tea with a Bedouin family in the desert or exploring the markets and souks of Amman, visitors to Jordan will experience a rich and vibrant culture that is both welcoming and inclusive.

In terms of practical information, the official language of Jordan is Arabic, although English is widely spoken in tourist areas. The local currency is the Jordanian Dinar (JOD), and credit cards are widely accepted in larger cities and tourist areas. Jordan is a safe and stable country, and visitors are encouraged to dress modestly and respect the customs and traditions.

Overall, Jordan is a fascinating and diverse country that offers something for everyone, from ancient historical sites to stunning natural landscapes and a rich and vibrant culture. Whether you're a first-time visitor or a seasoned traveler, Jordan is sure to leave a lasting impression and inspire you to return again and again.

History and Culture

Jordan has a rich history that dates back thousands of years. It is home to some of the world's most important historical and archaeological sites. This stunning city is carved entirely out of rock, and visitors can wander through its narrow canyons and marvel at its towering monuments and tombs.

The country is also home to the ruins of Jerash, a well-preserved Roman city that gives visitors a glimpse into what life was like during the Roman Empire. Visitors can explore the city's ancient temples, amphitheaters, and colonnaded streets.

Jordan is also steeped in culture, and visitors can experience it through traditional dance, music, and food. The country's capital, Amman, is a modern city with a vibrant arts and culture scene. It is home to several museums, galleries, and performance venues where visitors can immerse themselves in the local culture.

Why visit Jordan?

Jordan is a small but incredibly diverse country situated in the heart of the Middle East, offering visitors an unforgettable experience that is steeped in history, culture, and natural beauty. From ancient ruins and cities to stunning landscapes and welcoming locals, Jordan has something for everyone.

Stunning Landscapes

Jordan is home to some of the world's most stunning natural landscapes. The country's desert landscapes are particularly breathtaking, and visitors can explore them by taking a camel trek or a hot air balloon ride over the desert.

Jordan is also home to the Dead Sea, which is the lowest point on earth and is famous for its healing properties. Visitors can float effortlessly in the sea's salty waters and slather themselves in the mineral-rich mud that lines its shores.

For outdoor enthusiasts, Jordan offers plenty of opportunities for hiking, rock climbing, and other adventure sports. The country's Wadi Rum desert is a popular destination for hiking and rock climbing, while the Dana Biosphere Reserve offers visitors the chance to explore a stunning desert landscape teeming with wildlife.

Warm and Welcoming People

One of the things that visitors to Jordan often remark upon is the warmth and hospitality of the local people. Jordanians are known for their welcoming nature and their willingness to go out of their way to make visitors feel at home.

From the shopkeepers in the bustling souks to the Bedouin guides in the desert, Jordanians are always eager to share their country and their culture with visitors. This makes Jordan a particularly appealing destination for solo travelers or those who want to experience the country's culture up close.

Safe and Stable Destination

Despite its location in the Middle East, Jordan is considered a safe and stable destination for visitors. The country's government is stable and committed to maintaining a peaceful environment for both locals and visitors.

Jordan also has a well-developed tourism industry, with plenty of experienced tour operators and guides who can help visitors navigate the country safely and comfortably. In addition, the country has a strong security presence, and visitors can feel confident that their safety is a top priority.

Jordan is a place that should be on every traveler's bucket list. With its rich history and culture, stunning landscapes, warm and welcoming people, and safe and stable environment, it offers visitors an unforgettable experience that is both unique and rewarding.

Best Time to Visit

The best time to visit Jordan depends on the type of experience you are looking for. The country has a hot and dry desert climate, with long, hot summers and mild winters. Generally, the best time to visit is during the spring and fall months, when temperatures are more moderate.

Spring (March-May) is a great time to visit Jordan, as temperatures are mild and the landscape is lush and green. This is a great time to visit the country's many outdoor attractions, such as the Wadi Rum desert and the Dana

Biosphere Reserve. Spring is also a great time to visit the ancient city of Petra, as the temperatures are pleasant and the crowds are smaller than during the peak summer season.

Fall (September-November) is another great time to visit Jordan, as temperatures begin to cool down after the summer heat. This is a great time to visit the country's many cultural attractions, such as the Roman ruins of Jerash and the capital city of Amman. Fall is also a great time to visit the Dead Sea, as the temperatures are comfortable and the crowds are smaller than during the summer months.

Summer (June-August) is the peak tourist season in Jordan, and temperatures can be very hot, with temperatures often exceeding 40 degrees Celsius (104 degrees Fahrenheit). However, this is also the time when many festivals and cultural events take place, such as the Jerash Festival of Culture and Arts, which is held in July each year.

Winter (December-February) can be a good time to visit Jordan for those who don't mind the cooler temperatures. The country's desert landscapes can be particularly stunning in the winter, with snow-capped mountains and clear blue skies. However, some attractions may be closed or have limited opening hours during the winter months.

In summary, the best time to visit Jordan is during the spring or fall months, when temperatures are more moderate and the crowds are smaller. However, with careful planning and preparation, it is possible to visit Jordan during any season and have an enjoyable experience.

Planning Your Trip

If you're planning a trip to Jordan, here are some things to keep in mind to make the most of your experience:

Check the Entry Requirements: Before booking your trip, make sure to check the entry requirements for Jordan. Visitors from certain countries may need a visa to enter the country, while others may be eligible for a visa on arrival. Make sure to check the latest information on the website of the Jordanian embassy or consulate in your home country.

Choose the Right Time to Visit: As mentioned earlier, the best time to visit Jordan is during the spring or fall months when temperatures are more moderate. However, keep in mind that this is also the peak tourist season, so prices may be higher and attractions may be more crowded. If you don't mind the heat, visiting during the summer can also be a good option, as many cultural events take place during this time.

Plan Your Itinerary: Jordan has a lot to offer, so it's important to plan your itinerary carefully to make the most of your time there. Popular attractions include Petra, Wadi Rum, Jerash, the Dead Sea, and Amman. Make sure to factor in travel time between destinations, as well as time for rest and relaxation.

Choose Your Accommodation Wisely: There are a variety of accommodation options available in Jordan, ranging from luxury hotels to budget guesthouses. It's important to choose an accommodation that fits your needs and budget. If you're planning to visit Petra, consider staying in the nearby town of Wadi Musa, which has a variety of accommodation options.

Pack Appropriately: Jordan has a desert climate, so it's important to pack appropriate clothing and gear. This includes lightweight and breathable clothing, a hat, sunglasses, sunscreen, and comfortable walking shoes. If you're planning to visit the desert, consider packing a jacket or sweater for cooler evenings.

Respect the Local Culture: Jordan is a conservative Muslim country, remember to respect local customs and traditions. This includes dressing modestly, particularly in more conservative areas, and avoiding public displays of affection. It's also important to be respectful of local customs, such as removing your shoes before entering a mosque.

Book Tours and Activities in Advance: Jordan has a thriving tourism industry, so it's important to book tours and activities in advance, particularly during peak tourist season. Popular activities include guided tours of Petra and Wadi Rum, hot air balloon rides over the desert, and spa treatments at the Dead Sea.

Tips for Travelers

Here are some useful tips for travelers planning a trip to Jordan:

Carry Cash: While credit cards are accepted in many places in Jordan, it's always a good idea to carry cash, particularly in smaller towns and more remote areas. The Jordanian dinar is the official currency, but US dollars are also widely accepted.

Learn Some Basic Arabic: While many Jordanians speak English, learning a few basic Arabic phrases can go a long way in making connections with locals and showing respect for the local culture.

Dress Appropriately: Jordan is a conservative Muslim country, and it's important to dress appropriately, particularly in more conservative areas. This means covering the shoulders, chest, and knees, and avoiding tight or revealing clothing.

Stay Hydrated: Jordan has a desert climate, and it's important to drink plenty of water, particularly during the summer months. It's a good idea to carry a reusable water bottle and refill it regularly.

Respect Local Customs: Jordan has a rich cultural heritage, and it's important to be respectful of local customs and traditions. This includes removing shoes before entering a mosque, asking for permission before taking photos of locals, and avoiding public displays of affection.

Be Aware of Scams: Like any tourist destination, there may be scams targeting travelers in Jordan. Be cautious of overly friendly locals offering unsolicited help or asking for money, and always confirm prices before agreeing to any services or purchases.

Try Local Cuisine: Jordanian cuisine is a delicious mix of Middle Eastern and Mediterranean flavors, with specialties like hummus, falafel, and shawarma. Be sure to try some local dishes during your trip, and don't be afraid to ask locals for restaurant recommendations.

Be Mindful of the Environment: Jordan is home to many natural wonders, and it's important to be mindful of the environment while traveling. This includes avoiding littering, sticking to designated trails, and respecting wildlife and natural habitats.

Visa Requirements

Visa requirements for Jordan vary depending on your country of citizenship and the length and purpose of your stay in the country. Citizens of some countries are exempt from obtaining a visa for certain periods of time, while others must obtain a visa before entering Jordan.

Citizens of many countries, including the United States, Canada, and most European nations, are eligible for a visa on arrival at Jordanian airports and land borders.

It's important to note that the visa on arrival is not available to all travelers, and certain nationalities may be required to obtain a visa in advance. Additionally, travelers who are planning to work or study in Jordan may be required to obtain a different type of visa.

To obtain a visa in advance, travelers can apply online through the Jordanian government's eVisa system, or through a Jordanian embassy or consulate. The cost and processing time for a visa will vary depending on the type of visa and the embassy or consulate where the application is made.

It's important to check the latest visa requirements and regulations before traveling to Jordan, as they can change frequently. Additionally, travelers should ensure that their passport is valid for at least six months beyond the date of entry to Jordan.

Overall, while visa requirements for Jordan can be complex, the process of obtaining a visa is generally straightforward and can be easily navigated with proper planning and preparation. With the right visa in hand, travelers can enjoy all that Jordan has to offer, from its stunning historical sites to its beautiful natural landscapes.

Artemis Temple

Chapter 2

Transportation Options

Transportation options in Jordan have evolved significantly in recent years, making it easier and more convenient for locals and tourists alike to explore this beautiful country. From private car rentals to public buses and taxis, there are plenty of transportation options available for travelers to choose from.

Getting to Jordan

International Airports in Jordan

If you're planning a trip to Jordan, you'll need to know which airports are available to you. Luckily, Jordan is home to several international airports that offer a range of flights to destinations around the world. Here, we'll provide an overview of the top international airports in Jordan, as well as tips on how to get to the country from various locations around the globe.

Queen Alia International Airport (QAIA)

QAIA is the largest and busiest airport in Jordan, located in the capital city of Amman. The airport serves as the main gateway to the country, handling millions of passengers each year. QAIA is located approximately 35 km south of Amman, and there are several transportation options available for travelers arriving at the airport.

Taxi services are available at the airport, and visitors can book a taxi through the airport's official taxi service or use ride-hailing apps like Uber and Careem. Additionally, there are public buses available that run to and from the airport to various locations in Amman and other cities in Jordan.

QAIA offers flights to and from destinations all over the world, with major airlines such as Emirates, Turkish Airlines, and Royal Jordanian serving the airport. If you're flying to Jordan from North America, you may need to make a connecting flight in Europe or the Middle East before arriving at QAIA.

King Hussein International Airport (KHIA)

KHIA is located in the southern Jordanian city of Aqaba, near the border with Israel and Saudi Arabia. The airport offers a range of domestic and international flights, with airlines such as Ryanair, easyJet, and Jazeera Airways serving the airport.

If you're visiting the southern part of Jordan or planning to cross the border into Israel or Saudi Arabia, KHIA may be the most convenient airport for you. The airport is located just a few kilometers from Aqaba's city center, and taxis and ride-hailing apps are readily available for transportation to and from the airport.

Marka International Airport

Marka International Airport is a smaller airport located in the heart of Amman, primarily serving domestic flights within Jordan. The airport is located approximately 7 km from Amman's city center, making it a convenient option for travelers who need to get around the country quickly.

Flights from Marka International Airport are operated by Royal Jordanian and other regional airlines, and destinations include cities such as Aqaba, Petra, and the Dead Sea.

Tips for Getting to Jordan

If you're traveling to Jordan from outside the Middle East, you'll likely need to make a connecting flight in Europe or the Middle East before arriving in Jordan. Some of the major airlines that offer flights to Jordan include Emirates, Turkish Airlines, and Qatar Airways.

Once you arrive in Jordan, there are several transportation options available for getting around the country. Taxis and ride-hailing apps like Uber and Careem are widely available in major cities like Amman and Aqaba, and public transportation options like buses and trains are available for travel between cities.

In order to enter Jordan, visitors will need a valid passport and may also need to obtain a visa depending on their country of origin. Visitors from certain countries may be eligible for a visa on arrival, while others will need to apply for a visa in advance.

Jordan is a beautiful country with a rich history and culture, and its international airports make it easily accessible to travelers from around the world. Whether you're visiting Amman for business, exploring the ancient city of Petra, or relaxing by the Dead Sea, the airports in Jordan provide convenient transportation options for getting around the country.

Land borders

Jordan shares land borders with several countries, including Israel, Iraq, Syria, and Saudi Arabia. Each of these borders has its own regulations and requirements for crossing, so it's important to do your research and plan ahead if you're planning to cross into or out of Jordan by land.

The most commonly used land border for travelers entering Jordan is the Allenby Bridge/King Hussein Bridge, which connects the West Bank in Palestine to Jordan. This border crossing is open to foreign travelers and requires a valid passport and visa to enter Jordan. Visa on arrival is not available at this border, so it's important to obtain a visa in advance if needed.

There are also several land border crossings between Jordan and Syria, although these crossings are currently closed due to the ongoing conflict in Syria. Travelers are advised to avoid all travel to Syria until the situation improves.

Jordan shares two land borders with Iraq, at Trebil and Karama. These borders are currently closed to foreign travelers due to security concerns, and travel to Iraq is currently not recommended.

Jordan shares a land border with Saudi Arabia at the Al Omari Border Crossing. This border crossing is open to foreign travelers, but it's important to check the latest regulations and requirements before crossing, as they can change frequently.

In general, crossing land borders in Jordan can be a time-consuming process, and travelers should be prepared for long wait times and extensive security checks. It's also important to be aware of any potential safety concerns or travel advisories in the region before planning a trip.

Overall, while crossing land borders in Jordan can be challenging, it can also be a rewarding and exciting way to explore the country and its neighboring regions. With proper planning and preparation, travelers can navigate the border crossings safely and enjoy all that Jordan has to offer.

Getting Around

Jordan offers several transportation options for travelers, including buses, taxis, rental cars, and private drivers.

Buses are a popular and inexpensive option for traveling within Jordan. The country has a well-developed bus network that connects major cities and towns, and many buses are air-conditioned and comfortable. Some bus companies also offer overnight buses for longer journeys. However, it's important to note that buses can be crowded and may not always run on time, so it's important to build in extra time when planning your itinerary.

Taxis are another popular option for traveling within Jordan, and they are widely available in cities and towns. Taxis are generally affordable and offer a convenient way to get around, especially if you're traveling in a group or carrying luggage. However, it's important to agree on a price with the driver before getting in the taxi, as meters are not always used.

Rental cars are also available in Jordan, and they offer a great deal of flexibility and independence for travelers.

However, it's important to be aware of the driving conditions in Jordan, which can be challenging, especially in urban areas. Additionally, some roads may be unpaved or poorly maintained, so it's important to choose a vehicle that is appropriate for the conditions.

Private drivers are a popular option for travelers who want to explore Jordan in comfort and style. Private drivers can be arranged through tour companies or hotels, and they offer a great deal of flexibility and personal attention. However, private drivers can be expensive, so it's important to budget accordingly.

Overall, Jordan offers a range of transportation options for travelers, each with its own advantages and disadvantages. By choosing the transportation option that best suits your needs and budget, you can make the most of your time in Jordan and explore all that this beautiful country has to offer.

Chapter 3

Accommodations

Jordan is a beautiful and diverse country that offers a range of accommodations for travelers of all budgets and preferences. Visitors to Jordan have a wide range of accommodation options to choose from, including luxurious five-star hotels, budget-friendly guesthouses, and everything in between. Whether you're planning a romantic getaway, a family vacation, or a backpacking trip, you'll find accommodation that suits your needs and budget.

From the bustling capital city of Amman to the scenic desert landscapes of Wadi Rum, Jordan offers a diverse range of accommodations that cater to all types of travelers. Below are some of the top accommodation options in Jordan to help you plan your perfect trip.

Hotels

Hotels are the most common type of accommodation in Jordan. There are a variety of hotels to choose from, ranging from budget-friendly to high-end luxury. In general, hotels in Jordan offer comfortable rooms with basic amenities such as air conditioning, Wi-Fi, and a private bathroom. Some of the high-end hotels offer additional amenities such as swimming pools, spas, and restaurants.

If you are looking for a luxury hotel experience, some of the best options in Jordan include the Four Seasons Hotel Amman, the Kempinski Hotel Amman, and the Marriott Amman Hotel. These hotels offer world-class amenities and are located in some of the most scenic areas of the country.

For budget travelers, there are plenty of options as well. Some of the best budget hotels in Jordan include the Amman Pasha Hotel, the Cliff Hotel, and the Jordan Tower Hotel. These hotels offer basic amenities at affordable prices and are perfect for travelers who are looking to save money on accommodations.

Resorts

Jordan is home to several high-end resorts that offer a luxurious experience for travelers. These resorts are typically located in scenic areas such as the Dead Sea, Aqaba, and Petra. They offer a range of amenities such as swimming pools, spas, restaurants, and bars.

If you are looking for a luxurious resort experience in Jordan, some of the best options include the Kempinski Hotel Aqaba, the Movenpick Resort & Spa Dead Sea, and the Petra Marriott Hotel. These resorts offer world-class amenities and are located in some of the most beautiful areas of the country.

Bed and Breakfasts

Bed and Breakfasts are a great option for travelers who are looking for a more personalized experience. They offer a cozy and homely environment, often with a home-cooked breakfast included in the price. Bed and Breakfasts are typically located in residential areas, giving travelers a chance to experience the local culture and way of life.

Some of the best Bed and Breakfasts in Jordan include the Hidab Hotel, the Petra Moon Hotel, and the Beit Sitti Guesthouse. These accommodations offer a unique and personalized experience, making them a great option for travelers who are looking for something different.

Camping

Camping is a popular option for travelers who are looking to explore the natural beauty of Jordan. There are several campgrounds located throughout the country, offering basic amenities such as tents, sleeping bags, and access to a communal bathroom.

Some of the best camping options in Jordan include the Wadi Rum Bedouin Camp, the Eco Park Camping, and the Rum Stars Camp. These campgrounds offer a unique and adventurous experience, allowing travelers to explore the natural beauty of the country.

Jordan offers a range of accommodations for travelers of all budgets and preferences. From luxurious resorts to budget-friendly hostels, there is something for everyone in this beautiful country. When choosing an accommodation in Jordan, it is important to consider your budget, location, and amenities.

Budget friendly accommodations

There are many budget-friendly accommodations available in Jordan, ranging from hostels and guesthouses to budget hotels and apartments. Here are a few options to consider:

Hostels: Hostels are a popular option for budget-conscious travelers. They offer dormitory-style accommodations and shared facilities like kitchens, bathrooms, and common areas. Some popular hostels in Jordan include Sydney Hostel in Amman, Nomads Hostel in Wadi Musa, and Jordan Tower Hotel in Amman.

Guesthouses: Guesthouses are another great option for budget travelers. They offer private rooms with shared facilities, and are often located in more residential neighborhoods. Some popular guesthouses in Jordan include Rafiki Hostel in Amman, Petra Moon Hotel in Wadi Musa, and Haddad Guesthouse in Madaba.

Budget hotels: There are many budget hotels in Jordan that offer basic amenities like air conditioning, Wi-Fi, and private bathrooms. Some popular budget hotels include Al-Houriat Hotel in Amman, Al-Anbat Midtown Hotel in Wadi Musa, and Madaba Hotel in Madaba.

Apartments: If you're traveling with a group or plan to stay in Jordan for an extended period of time, renting an apartment can be a cost-effective option. Many apartments are fully furnished and come with amenities like kitchens and Wi-Fi.

Chapter 4

Jordan's Top Destinations

Petra

Petra, one of the world's most magnificent ancient cities located in the southwestern desert of Jordan. This UNESCO World Heritage Site is also known as the "Rose City" due to its reddish-pink sandstone cliffs that were hand-carved into stunning temples, tombs, and other grand structures.

Attracting millions of visitors each year, Petra is a popular destination for history buffs, archaeologists, and nature enthusiasts. If you're planning a trip to Petra, we've got you covered with this ultimate guide to the Rose City.

Getting to Petra

Petra is located in the southern part of Jordan, and the nearest airport is Queen Alia International Airport (AMM) in Amman. From there, you can take a taxi or bus to Petra, which is approximately a three-hour drive. Alternatively, you can take a domestic flight to King Hussein International Airport in Aqaba, which is closer to Petra, and then drive or take a taxi.

Exploring Petra

Petra is a vast ancient city, and you'll need at least two full days to explore it properly. The main entrance to Petra is through the Siq, a narrow gorge that winds its way for over a kilometer, providing a stunning entrance to the city.

Once inside, you'll be greeted with magnificent structures carved out of the sandstone cliffs, including the Treasury, the Monastery, the Royal Tombs, and the Great Temple, among others. You can also explore the ancient Roman-style amphitheater, which could seat over 8,000 spectators.

Hiking and Trekking

One of the best ways to experience Petra is on foot, and there are several hiking and trekking trails that you can take. The most popular hike is to the Monastery, which is located at the top of a hill and requires climbing over 800 steps. The view from the top is breathtaking, and you'll be rewarded with stunning panoramic views of the surrounding landscape.

Another popular trail is the Al Khubtha Trail, which takes you to the High Place of Sacrifice, an ancient altar that was used for sacrifices in ancient times. This trail offers incredible views of Petra and the surrounding mountains.

Accommodation

There are several accommodation options in Petra, including hotels, guesthouses, and camping sites. If you're looking for a luxurious experience, there are several high-end hotels that offer stunning views of Petra, including the Petra Marriott Hotel and the Mövenpick Resort Petra.

For budget travelers, there are several guesthouses and camping sites that offer basic amenities at affordable prices. One of the most popular camping sites is the Bedouin campsite, which offers a unique experience of sleeping in a traditional Bedouin tent under the starry desert sky.

Food and Drinks

Petra offers a variety of dining options, including traditional Jordanian cuisine, Mediterranean cuisine, and international cuisine. There are several restaurants and cafes located in and around Petra, offering a range of dishes to suit every palate.

One of the most popular dishes in Jordan is Mansaf, a traditional Jordanian dish made of lamb cooked in a yogurt sauce and served with rice. Another popular dish is Zarb, which is a Bedouin-style barbecue that is cooked underground and served with rice and vegetables.

Shopping

Petra is known for its traditional handicrafts, including pottery, ceramics, and jewelry. You can find several shops and markets located in and around Petra, offering a range of traditional handicrafts to take home as souvenirs.

The most popular shopping area in Petra is the Siq, where you can find several vendors selling traditional handicrafts and souvenirs.

Best Time to Visit

The best time to visit Petra is from March to May and from September to November; this period, the weather is mild and comfortable. During the summer months, the temperatures can reach up to 40°C, making it challenging to explore the city during the day.

During the winter months, Petra can experience occasional snowfall, which can make hiking and trekking trails difficult to navigate. However, if you're up for a winter adventure, Petra can be a magical sight covered in snow.

Tips for Visiting Petra

Here are some tips to help you make the most of your visit to Petra:

Wear comfortable shoes and clothing, as you'll be doing a lot of walking and hiking.

Carry plenty of water and snacks, as there are limited food and drink options inside Petra.

Hire a guide to help you navigate Petra and learn more about its history and significance.

Try to visit Petra early in the morning or late in the afternoon to avoid the crowds and the heat.

Respect the local culture and customs, and dress appropriately when visiting religious sites.

Petra is a unique and magical destination that offers a blend of ancient history, stunning natural beauty, and modern amenities.

Wadi Rum

This is located in southern Jordan, near the border with Saudi Arabia. It is part of the larger Wadi Rum Protected Area, which covers over 700 square kilometers of desert landscape.

Wadi Rum, a majestic desert in Jordan that has been mesmerizing travelers for centuries. We are excited to take you on a journey through this enchanting destination, known for its stunning landscape, unique culture, and rich history.

Landscape

The first thing that comes to mind when thinking about Wadi Rum is its breathtaking landscape. This desert is home to some of the most spectacular rock formations, sandstone arches, and towering cliffs in the world. It is a photographer's paradise, with the changing light of day and night casting an ever-shifting play of shadows and hues on the vast expanse of sand and rocks.

The desert of Wadi Rum is also famous for its red sand dunes, which are an iconic feature of the area. These dunes are formed from the erosion of sandstone cliffs, and their rich red color contrasts beautifully with the blue skies and golden sunlight. Walking or hiking through the dunes is an experience like no other, with the silence and stillness of the desert enveloping you in a sense of calm and peace.

Culture

Wadi Rum is also known for its unique culture and way of life. The local Bedouin people have been living in this desert for generations, and they have developed a deep connection to the land and its natural rhythms. They are known for their hospitality and generosity, and many travelers who visit Wadi Rum are struck by the warmth and kindness of the Bedouin people.

One of the amazing ways to experience the local culture is to stay in a Bedouin camp. These camps are scattered throughout the desert, and they offer a chance to sleep under the stars, enjoy traditional Bedouin food, and learn about the customs and traditions of the local people. Some camps even offer camel rides or Jeep tours, which are a fun way to explore the desert and see some of its most stunning sights.

History

Wadi Rum is also steeped in history, with evidence of human habitation dating back thousands of years. The Nabataean people, who famously built the city of Petra, also had a presence in Wadi Rum, and their influence can still be seen in the many rock carvings and inscriptions that dot the desert landscape. In more recent times, Wadi Rum was used as a base for Lawrence of Arabia during the Arab Revolt against the Ottoman Empire, and his legacy can still be felt in the area today.

Exploring Wadi Rum

There are many ways to explore Wadi Rum, and the best way depends on your interests and preferences. Some people choose to hike through the desert on their own, while others prefer to take a guided tour. Jeep tours are a popular option, as they allow you to cover a lot of ground and see many of the desert's most famous landmarks in a short amount of time. Camel rides are another popular option, and they offer a slower, more traditional way to explore the desert.

No matter how you choose to explore Wadi Rum, there are some sights that you simply can't miss. The Seven Pillars of Wisdom, which were famously described by Lawrence of Arabia, are a must-see for any visitor to the area. These towering rock formations rise up out of the desert floor, and their sheer size and scale are awe-inspiring.

Another must-see sight is the Burdah Rock Bridge, which is one of the largest natural arches in the world. This sandstone arch spans a deep ravine, and the views from the top are simply stunning

There are also many other rock formations and landmarks that are worth exploring in Wadi Rum, such as the Khazali Canyon, the Lawrence's Spring, and the Um Fruth Rock Bridge. Each of these landmarks has its own unique history and significance, and they all contribute to the magic and wonder of this beautiful desert.

When planning your visit to Wadi Rum, it is important to keep in mind the weather and the best time to visit. The summer months can be extremely hot, with temperatures soaring above 40°C (104°F), so it is best to visit in the cooler months between October and April. During this time, the weather is mild and pleasant, and the desert landscape is at its most beautiful.

In terms of accommodation, there are many options to choose from in Wadi Rum, ranging from luxury camps to basic Bedouin tents. Many of the camps offer traditional Bedouin food and hospitality, and some even have hot showers and Wi-Fi. It is important to research and book your accommodation in advance, especially during peak travel season, to ensure that you have the best possible experience.

Wadi Rum is a truly magical destination that offers something for everyone. Whether you are a nature lover, a history buff, or simply seeking an escape from the hustle and bustle of modern life, this desert is sure to leave you feeling inspired and rejuvenated.

Dead Sea

The Dead Sea is situated between Jordan to the east and Israel and Palestine to the west; it is a saltwater lake known for its high salt and mineral content. It is the lowest point on Earth, with a surface level of 430 meters below sea level.

It is a popular tourist destination due to its unique features, including its buoyancy-enhancing properties that allow swimmers to float effortlessly on its surface. The high salt content of the water also makes it impossible for fish and other marine life to survive, which has contributed to the lake's name.

In addition to its recreational value, the Dead Sea is also famous for its therapeutic benefits. The mineral-rich mud and salt deposits found along the shore are believed to have healing properties for skin conditions, arthritis, and respiratory illnesses.

Visitors to the Dead Sea can enjoy a variety of activities, such as sunbathing, swimming, and mud baths. The area is also home to several spas and resorts that offer a range of health and beauty treatments utilizing the natural resources of the lake.

When planning a trip to the Dead Sea, it's important to note that the area's extreme climate can be challenging, with hot and dry summers and mild winters. It's essential to stay hydrated and use sunscreen to protect your skin from the strong sun.

In addition to the recreational and therapeutic offerings, the Dead Sea region also has a rich history and culture. The area has been inhabited for thousands of years, with evidence of human settlements dating back to the Neolithic period.

Visitors can explore archaeological sites such as the ancient city of Jericho, which is believed to be one of the oldest continuously inhabited cities in the world. Other notable historical and cultural sites include the Qumran Caves, where the famous Dead Sea Scrolls were discovered, and the Masada fortress, a UNESCO World Heritage site.

For those interested in outdoor activities, the Dead Sea region offers a variety of hiking trails, including the Israel National Trail, which passes through the area. The unique landscape, which includes rugged mountains and barren deserts, provides a stunning backdrop for adventure seekers.

In terms of accommodations, the Dead Sea region has a range of options to suit different budgets and preferences. From luxurious resorts to rustic campsites, visitors can find accommodation that meets their needs. Many hotels and resorts also offer direct access to the Dead Sea and its therapeutic mud and salt deposits.

When visiting the Dead Sea, it's important to be aware of the environmental concerns surrounding the area. The lake is shrinking at an alarming rate due to overuse of its water resources for industrial and agricultural purposes, as well as the diversion of its main source of water, the Jordan River. As a result, the Dead Sea is becoming increasingly salty and its shoreline is receding, causing environmental and economic damage to the surrounding areas.

To address these issues, there are ongoing efforts to conserve and protect the Dead Sea. These include plans to build a pipeline from the Red Sea to the Dead Sea, which would provide much-needed water resources to the area while also stabilizing the lake's water levels.

Visitors can also do their part to help protect the environment by being mindful of their water usage and waste disposal while in the region. Simple actions such as taking shorter showers and properly disposing of trash can go a long way in preserving this natural wonder for future generations.

The Dead Sea is a unique and fascinating destination that offers visitors a chance to experience a natural wonder unlike anywhere else on Earth. With its recreational, therapeutic, historical, and cultural offerings, there is something for everyone to enjoy. As we explore this magnificent area, let us also remember to be responsible travelers and do our part to protect the environment and preserve this natural treasure for generations to come.

Amman

Discovering the wonders of Amman, the capital city of Jordan, is a must-do for any traveler. With its rich history, culture, and modern amenities, Amman is a fascinating destination that caters to all types of visitors.

Historical Sites

Amman's rich history is evident in its many ancient sites and landmarks that showcase the city's past. One of the most popular attractions in Amman is the Roman Theater, which dates back to the 2nd century AD. The theater is a magnificent structure that can seat up to 6,000 people and is still used for cultural events today. Nearby, the Roman Nymphaeum is a beautiful fountain that was once the city's main source of water.

Another must-see historical site in Amman is the Citadel, which sits atop Jabal al-Qala'a hill and provides panoramic views of the city. The Citadel contains many ancient ruins, including the Umayyad Palace, the Temple of Hercules, and the Byzantine Church. History buffs will also enjoy visiting the Jordan Museum, which houses a vast collection of artifacts from the country's history, including the Dead Sea Scrolls.

Culture

Amman's culture is a blend of traditional and modern influences, and visitors can experience this unique fusion through the city's art, music, and cuisine. One of the best places to immerse yourself in Amman's culture is Rainbow Street, a lively area with many cafes, restaurants, and shops. Here, you can try local dishes like mansaf, a traditional Jordanian dish made with lamb, rice, and yogurt sauce.

For music lovers, the Al Balad Music Festival is a must-attend event. The festival takes place in downtown Amman and showcases local and international musicians playing a variety of genres, from jazz to Arabic music. Art enthusiasts can visit the Darat Al Funun art gallery, which displays contemporary art from the Arab world and beyond.

Outdoor Adventures

Amman is also a great destination for outdoor enthusiasts, with plenty of opportunities for activities such as biking, hiking, and other outdoor activities. For those seeking adventure, the Jordan Trail is a 400-mile-long hiking trail that stretches from the north of Jordan to the south. The trail takes hikers through some of Jordan's most stunning landscapes, including mountains, deserts, and canyons.

Visitors can also enjoy horseback riding, rock climbing, and hot air balloon rides in Amman.

Amman is a fascinating city with various outdoor adventures. From exploring ancient sites and sampling local cuisine to attending cultural festivals and hiking through stunning landscapes, there's something for everyone in Amman.

Where to Stay

Amman has a range of accommodation options to suit all budgets and preferences. The city has many high-end hotels, including the Four Seasons Hotel Amman, the St. Regis Amman, and the Grand Hyatt Amman. These hotels offer luxurious amenities, including spas, fitness centers, and rooftop pools.

For those on a budget, Amman also has many affordable guesthouses and hostels, such as the Jordan Tower Hotel and the Art Hotel Downtown. These accommodations are often located in the heart of the city and provide a comfortable and convenient base for exploring Amman.

Getting Around

Getting around Amman is easy, thanks to the city's extensive public transportation network. The city has a modern bus system, which is inexpensive and convenient for getting around the city. Visitors can also use ride-hailing services like Uber and Careem to get around.

For those who prefer to explore on foot, Amman is a pedestrian-friendly city with many pedestrian-only streets and sidewalks. Walking is a great way to discover the city's hidden gems and soak up its vibrant atmosphere.

Amman is a city that should not be missed by any traveler. With its rich history, vibrant culture, and stunning natural landscapes, Amman offers something for everyone. Whether you're a history buff, a foodie, or an outdoor enthusiast, you'll find plenty to see and do in this incredible city.

Aqaba

Aqaba, the hidden gem of Jordan, where sun-kissed beaches, pristine waters, and a rich history await you. Nestled on the coast of the Red Sea, Aqaba is a popular tourist destination for those seeking adventure, relaxation, and culture.

Aqaba's Beaches

Aqaba is home to some of the most beautiful beaches in the world, with crystal clear waters and stunning views of the surrounding mountains. The most popular beach in Aqaba is the South Beach, which is located in the heart of the city and is easily accessible. It's a great spot to relax, sunbathe, and enjoy the beautiful scenery. If you're looking for something more secluded, head to the Coral Beach Nature Reserve, which is a protected area that is home to some of the most vibrant coral reefs in the world.

History

Aqaba is a city steeped in history, with a rich cultural heritage that dates back thousands of years. One of the most popular attractions in Aqaba is the Aqaba Fort, which was built by the Mamluk Sultanate in the 14th century. The fort has been restored and is now home to a museum that showcases Aqaba's history and culture. Another must-visit site is the ancient city of Ayla, which was founded in the 7th century and was once a major trading center.

Natural Wonders

Aqaba is home to a number of natural wonders that are just waiting to be explored. The Wadi Rum desert is a must-visit for those who love adventure, with its breathtaking landscapes and rugged terrain. You can explore the desert by jeep or camel, and even spend the night in a Bedouin tent under the stars. For those who prefer the water, the Red Sea is home to some of the world's most diverse and beautiful marine life. You can go snorkeling or scuba diving and explore the coral reefs and colorful fish that call the Red Sea home.

Culinary Delights

No visit to Aqaba is complete without indulging in the local cuisine. Aqaba is home to a number of delicious restaurants that serve up traditional Jordanian dishes, as well as international cuisine. One of the most popular local dishes is mansaf, which is made with lamb, rice, and a yogurt-based sauce. Another must-try dish is falafel, which is made with chickpeas and is a popular street food in Aqaba.

Aqaba is a hidden gem that offers something for everyone, whether you're looking for adventure, relaxation, or culture. With its beautiful beaches, rich history, natural wonders, and delicious cuisine, Aqaba is a must-visit destination for anyone traveling to Jordan.

Getting to Aqaba

Getting to Aqaba is easy, with the city being accessible by air, land, and sea. The nearest airport is King Hussein International Airport, which is located just outside the city center. From the airport, you can take a taxi or bus to your hotel or destination. If you're traveling by car, Aqaba is easily accessible from other parts of Jordan, with well-maintained highways connecting the city to Amman and other major cities. Finally, Aqaba is also a popular destination for cruise ships, with many international cruise lines stopping in the city.

Best Time to Visit

The best time to visit Aqaba is during the spring and fall months, when the weather is mild and comfortable. Summers in Aqaba can be hot and dry, with temperatures reaching up to 40°C (104°F), so it's important to stay hydrated and protect yourself from the sun if you're visiting during this time. Winters in Aqaba are mild, with temperatures averaging around 20°C (68°F), making it a great time to visit if you prefer cooler weather.

Where to Stay

Aqaba has a variety of accommodation options to suit all budgets and preferences. If you're looking for luxury, there are several high-end resorts that offer world-class amenities and services. For those on a budget, there are also plenty of affordable hotels and hostels that offer comfortable and clean rooms. No matter where you choose to stay in Aqaba, you're sure to enjoy the city's warm hospitality and friendly atmosphere.

Aqaba is a destination that truly has something for everyone, from beach lovers to history buffs to adventure seekers

Jerash

Jerash is a historical city located in the northwestern part of Jordan, approximately 48 kilometers north of the capital, Amman. The city is famous for its well-preserved ancient ruins and is considered one of the best examples of Roman architecture outside of Italy.

History

The history of Jerash dates back to the Neolithic period, but the city flourished under the rule of the Roman Empire in the 1st century AD. It was then known as Gerasa and was an important center of trade and commerce in the region. The city was also renowned for its impressive monuments, including the Temple of Artemis, the Arch of Hadrian, and the Oval Plaza.

Today, visitors can explore the ruins of Jerash and witness the city's remarkable architecture and engineering feats. The highlights include the impressive South Theatre, which could seat over 3000 people, and the Cardo Maximus, the main avenue that runs through the city. Visitors can also see the impressive Hadrian's Arch, which was built to commemorate the visit of the Roman Emperor Hadrian to the city.

In addition to the ancient ruins, Jerash is also home to a number of modern amenities, including restaurants, cafes, and souvenir shops. Visitors can enjoy traditional Jordanian cuisine and shop for souvenirs, including traditional handicrafts and local spices.

Apart from exploring the ancient ruins, visitors to Jerash can also participate in various cultural and recreational activities. The annual Jerash Festival is a popular event that takes place in July and features performances by local and international artists, including traditional music, dance, and theater.

Another attraction is the Ajloun Forest Reserve, located approximately 13 kilometers from Jerash. The reserve is home to a wide variety of flora and fauna, including oak trees, wild boars, and wolves. Visitors can hike on the many trails, enjoy a picnic, or even camp overnight in the reserve.

Whether you're interested in history, culture, or nature, Jerash offers something for everyone. Its ancient ruins, modern amenities, and proximity to other popular attractions make it a must-visit destination in Jordan.

One of the best times to visit Jerash is in the spring or fall when the weather is mild and pleasant. Summer temperatures can be quite hot, so visitors should plan accordingly and bring sunscreen, hats, and plenty of water.

Visitors to Jerash can also take advantage of the city's many guided tours and informative audio guides, which provide a deeper understanding of the history and significance of the various monuments and structures.

In addition, Jerash is a relatively safe and welcoming destination for tourists. The local people are friendly and hospitable, and the city has a low crime rate. However, visitors should still exercise common sense and take precautions to safeguard their belongings and personal safety.

When visiting Jerash, remember to respect local customs and traditions.

Getting Around

In terms of transportation, visitors to Jerash can take a taxi or public bus from Amman. Many tours and private transportation options are also available.

For those interested in staying overnight in Jerash, there are a variety of accommodation options available, including hotels, guesthouses, and camping facilities. Some of the hotels offer stunning views of the ancient ruins, making for a truly unique experience.

Jerash is a destination with a blend of history, culture, and natural beauty. With its well-preserved ancient ruins, modern amenities, and welcoming people, it is a must-visit destination for anyone traveling to Jordan.

Madaba

Madaba is a small city in Jordan, known for its rich cultural heritage and historical significance. With a population of around 60,000 people, Madaba has become a popular destination for tourists from all over the world. The city's history dates back to biblical times, and it is famous for its exquisite mosaics that depict various scenes from religious and cultural events.

The city of Madaba is located about 30 kilometers southwest of Amman, the capital city of Jordan. It is situated on a plateau, which offers stunning views of the surrounding landscape. Madaba's location makes it an excellent base for tourists who want to explore the many attractions that Jordan has to offer.

History and Culture

Madaba's history dates back to biblical times, and it is mentioned in the Old Testament as the city of Medeba. The city played a vital role in the early Christian era and was an important center for religious pilgrimage. Madaba is famous for its stunning mosaics that depict various scenes from religious and cultural events.

The most famous of these mosaics is the Madaba Map, which is located in the Greek Orthodox Church of St. George. The Madaba Map is the oldest known map of the Holy Land and dates back to the 6th century. The map depicts the Holy Land and Jerusalem, and it is considered to be one of the most important and valuable mosaics in the world.

Apart from the Madaba Map, the city has many other significant mosaics, including the Church of the Apostles, the Church of the Virgin Mary, and the Church of the Holy

Sepulcher. These mosaics depict various scenes from the Bible and are a testament to the city's rich cultural heritage.

Things to See and Do

Madaba has many attractions for tourists to explore. The city's ancient history and rich cultural heritage make it a fascinating destination for history buffs and art enthusiasts. Here are some of the top things to see and do in Madaba:

Visit the Madaba Map: The Madaba Map is undoubtedly the city's most famous attraction and a must-visit for anyone interested in history and art. The mosaic is located in the Greek Orthodox Church of St. George, and visitors can marvel at its exquisite details and intricate design.

Explore the Archaeological Park: The Archaeological Park is a vast complex of ancient ruins that date back to the Hellenistic and Roman periods. The park covers an area of around 7 hectares and includes the remains of several temples, a theater, and a Byzantine-era church.

Visit the Church of the Apostles: The Church of the Apostles is located in the heart of Madaba and is famous for its stunning mosaics that depict various scenes from the

Bible. The church is believed to have been built in the 6th century and is one of the oldest Christian churches in the city.

Explore the City Center: The city center of Madaba is a vibrant and bustling area with many shops, restaurants, and cafes. Visitors can stroll through the narrow streets and alleyways and take in the sights and sounds of the city.

Visit the Madaba Institute for Mosaic Art and Restoration

The Madaba Institute for Mosaic Art and Restoration is a world-renowned center for the restoration and preservation of mosaics. Visitors can take a tour of the institute and see the experts at work.

Madaba is a city full of history and culture, with many attractions for tourists to explore. The city's ancient ruins, stunning mosaics, and vibrant city center make it a fascinating destination for anyone interested in history, art, and culture. Whether you're a solo traveler, a family, or a group of friends, Madaba has something to offer for everyone.

One of the best things about Madaba is that it's an affordable destination, and visitors can enjoy a fantastic experience without breaking the bank. The city's hotels and restaurants cater to a variety of budgets, and visitors can enjoy local cuisine at reasonable prices.

Madaba is a charming and enchanting city full of history and culture. Its ancient ruins, stunning mosaics, and vibrant city center make it a place to be for anyone interested in history, art, and culture. With affordable prices and friendly locals, Madaba is an excellent destination for solo travelers, families, and groups of friends.

Mount Nebo

Mount Nebo is a historic site located in Jordan, and is said to be the place where Moses saw the Promised Land. This site is not only of religious significance, but it also boasts stunning views of the Dead Sea, the Jordan River Valley, and the surrounding mountains.

Getting to Mount Nebo

Mount Nebo is located in Madaba, Jordan, and is easily accessible by car or taxi. The journey from Amman, the capital city of Jordan, to Mount Nebo takes approximately

30-40 minutes by car, depending on traffic. If you do not have access to a car, taxis are readily available for hire. Alternatively, many tour operators offer day trips to Mount Nebo, which include transportation and a guided tour.

Exploring Mount Nebo

Upon arrival, visitors are greeted by a large statue of Moses, welcoming them to the site. As you walk further into the site, you will come across the Memorial Church of Moses, which was built in the 4th century AD. This church is home to stunning mosaics that date back to the Byzantine era, and are some of the oldest in the world. The mosaics depict various scenes from the Bible, and are a must-see for any art or history enthusiast.

After exploring the church, visitors can head to the Mount Nebo Interpretation Centre, which offers a wealth of information about the site's history and significance. The center has a range of exhibits and multimedia displays that provide visitors with a deeper understanding of Mount Nebo and its importance.

Once you have finished exploring the interpretation center, be sure to head outside to take in the breathtaking views of the surrounding area. On a clear day, visitors can see as far as Jerusalem and Bethlehem, making it an ideal spot for photography and relaxation.

Tips for visiting Mount Nebo

Wear comfortable shoes, as the site involves a fair amount of walking

Bring sunscreen and a hat, as the sun can be quite strong in the summer months

If you are visiting during the peak season (May-September), be prepared for large crowds

Respect the site's religious significance and dress modestly

Bring plenty of water, as there are limited options for purchasing drinks on site

Mount Nebo is a must-visit destination for anyone traveling to Jordan. Its rich history, stunning mosaics, and breathtaking views make it a truly unique and unforgettable experience.

Mount Nebo is also home to a range of hiking trails, which offer visitors the chance to explore the surrounding mountains and valleys. These trails range from easy to moderate difficulty, and are suitable for all ages and fitness levels. Some of the most popular trails include the Mount Nebo to Madaba Trail, which takes approximately four hours to complete and offers stunning views of the surrounding area.

For those who are interested in learning more about the local culture, the nearby town of Madaba is home to a range of traditional crafts, including pottery, weaving, and glassblowing. Visitors can explore local markets and workshops to see these crafts being made by skilled artisans.

When it comes to accommodation, there are a range of options available in and around Mount Nebo, from luxury hotels to budget-friendly guesthouses. Many of these accommodations offer stunning views of the surrounding area and easy access to the hiking trails and other attractions.

Visiting Mount Nebo is an unforgettable experience that offers a unique insight into the history and culture of Jordan.

Dana Biosphere Reserve

This is a protected area located in southern Jordan. It covers an area of 320 square kilometers and is home to a diverse range of plant and animal species. The reserve is characterized by its rugged terrain, deep valleys, and towering cliffs, making it a popular destination for hiking and adventure tourism.

The Dana Biosphere Reserve is home to over 700 species of plants, 215 species of birds, and 38 species of mammals, including the endangered Nubian ibex and sand cat. The reserve also contains important archaeological sites, including ancient copper mines and the ruins of a Byzantine monastery.

Visitors to the reserve can take guided tours, go hiking or mountain biking, and stay in eco-friendly lodges that have been built to minimize the impact on the environment. The Dana Biosphere Reserve is a unique and beautiful destination that offers visitors the opportunity to experience Jordan's natural beauty and cultural heritage.

The reserve is located in the midst of the Jordan Rift Valley and encompasses a range of landscapes, including rocky mountains, sand dunes, and wadis. The Dana Village, located at the entrance of the reserve, is a traditional village that has been preserved and restored, giving visitors a glimpse into rural life in Jordan.

One of the most popular activities in the reserve is hiking, with a range of trails available for visitors of different skill levels. The most famous of these is the Dana to Petra trek, which takes several days and passes through stunning landscapes and archaeological sites.

The reserve also offers opportunities for birdwatching, with some of the most sought-after species including the Syrian Serin, Tristram's Starling, and the Lappet-faced Vulture. Visitors can also take part in cultural activities such as bread-making and weaving workshops, allowing them to learn about traditional Jordanian culture and support local communities.

The Dana Biosphere Reserve is a model for sustainable tourism in Jordan, with a focus on eco-friendly practices and community involvement. The reserve provides employment opportunities for local communities and contributes to the conservation of Jordan's natural and cultural heritage.

The Dana Biosphere Reserve is also home to several important archaeological sites, including the ruins of the ancient copper mines of Wadi Feinan, which date back to the Bronze Age. The Byzantine monastery of Saint Lot is another notable site, which is perched on a hill overlooking the valley and offers stunning views.

One of the key initiatives is the Dana Guest House, an eco-friendly lodge that was established to provide sustainable tourism opportunities and support local communities. The guest house employs local staff, uses locally sourced products, and has implemented a range of measures to reduce its environmental impact.

Overall, the Dana Biosphere Reserve is a unique and valuable destination in Jordan, offering visitors the opportunity to experience the country's natural beauty, cultural heritage, and commitment to sustainable development.

Chapter 5

Food and Drink

Jordan is a country known for its rich history, vibrant culture, and stunning landscapes. But it's also a destination for food lovers looking to discover the unique flavors of traditional Jordanian cuisine. From fragrant spices to succulent meats and fresh vegetables, Jordanian food is a feast for the senses.

Traditional Cuisine

Jordanian cuisine is a reflection of the country's diverse cultural influences, geography, and history. It has been influenced by the Bedouin, Arab, and Ottoman cultures. The dishes are hearty, flavorful, and rely on simple yet bold flavors. Jordanian cuisine is characterized by the use of fresh and seasonal ingredients, spices, and herbs that are essential to its unique taste.

Mansaf: The National Dish

Mansaf is considered the national dish of Jordan and is a must-try for any food enthusiast. This dish consists of tender lamb or goat meat cooked in a yogurt sauce and served on a bed of rice with almonds and pine nuts. The dish is traditionally served on a large platter and shared with family and friends.

Falafel: A Vegetarian Delight

Falafel is a vegetarian dish that has gained immense popularity worldwide, and Jordan is no exception. This dish is made of ground chickpeas mixed with herbs and spices, formed into small balls, and deep-fried. Falafel is typically served with pita bread, hummus, and tahini sauce. It's a healthy and satisfying meal that can be enjoyed as a snack or a main dish.

Makloubeh: A One-Pot Wonder

Makloubeh is a one-pot dish that is a staple in Jordanian households. It's a hearty dish made with layers of rice, vegetables, and meat that are cooked together to form a delicious casserole. The dish gets its name from the Arabic word "makloubeh," which means "upside-down" as the casserole is served upside down on a platter.

Jordanian Salads: Fresh and Flavorful

Jordanian salads are a perfect accompaniment to any meal, and they are an essential part of traditional Jordanian cuisine. These salads are made with fresh and seasonal ingredients, such as tomatoes, cucumbers, onions, and parsley, and dressed with lemon juice, olive oil, and sumac.

Za'atar: The King of Spices

Za'atar is a blend of herbs and spices that is used in many Jordanian dishes. The blend typically consists of dried thyme, oregano, marjoram, sesame seeds, and sumac. Za'atar is sprinkled on bread, used as a seasoning for meats and vegetables, and can be mixed with olive oil to make a dip.

Traditional Jordanian cuisine is a gastronomic adventure that will leave you wanting more. From hearty meat dishes to fresh and flavorful salads, Jordanian cuisine is a celebration of the country's rich cultural heritage.

Popular dishes to try

Here are some additional dishes that you might enjoy:

Kofta: Kofta is a grilled meat dish made of ground beef or lamb, mixed with herbs and spices, and shaped into small sausages or meatballs. It's typically served with rice, salad, and flatbread.

Shawarma: Shawarma is a popular street food in Jordan and throughout the Middle East. It consists of thin slices of marinated meat (usually chicken or lamb) that are roasted on a spit and served in a pita bread with vegetables and tahini sauce.

Musakhan: Musakhan is a traditional Palestinian dish that is also popular in Jordan. It consists of roasted chicken or lamb, sautéed onions, and sumac, all served on top of flatbread.

Maqluba: Maqluba is a dish that translates to "upside-down" in Arabic, and it's similar to makloubeh. It's a one-pot dish that features layers of rice, vegetables, and meat that are cooked together and then flipped upside down onto a platter before serving.

Kunafa: Kunafa is a popular dessert in Jordan and throughout the Middle East. It consists of a layer of crispy phyllo dough, a layer of sweet cheese, and a layer of syrup made from sugar and rosewater.

Zarb: Zarb is a Bedouin dish that is cooked underground. It consists of chicken, lamb, or goat that is marinated with spices and then buried in a pit with hot coals and covered with sand. After several hours, the meat is tender and flavorful and served with rice, vegetables, and bread.

Maglouba: Maglouba is similar to maqluba, but it's a bit different in terms of preparation. This dish consists of layers of rice, vegetables, and meat that are cooked together and then flipped over onto a platter before serving.

Fatayer: Fatayer are small, triangular pastries that are filled with spinach, cheese, or meat. They're a popular snack in Jordan and can be found at bakeries and markets throughout the country.

Mansaf: Mansaf is a traditional Jordanian dish that is often served at special occasions such as weddings and festivals. It consists of rice, lamb or chicken, and a yogurt sauce called jameed. Mansaf is usually eaten with the hands and is a delicious and satisfying meal.

Fattoush: Fattoush is a salad made with cucumbers, lettuce, onions, tomatoes, and parsley, all tossed in a lemony dressing and topped with crispy pieces of pita bread. It's a refreshing and healthy dish that's perfect for a light lunch or dinner.

These dishes are just a small sampling of the rich and diverse cuisine that Jordan has to offer. Whether you're a seasoned foodie or just looking to try something new, there's no shortage of delicious options to explore in Jordanian cuisine. From hearty stews and grilled meats to fresh salads and sweet pastries, there's something for every palate in this vibrant and flavorful cuisine.

Dining Options

Jordan offers a wide range of dining options, from casual street food stalls and local markets to high-end restaurants and cafes. Here are some of the top dining options to check out when visiting Jordan:

Street food: Street food is a popular dining option in Jordan and can be found throughout the country. Some of the most popular street foods include falafel, shawarma, hummus, and fresh fruit juices. You can find street vendors selling these delicious snacks in markets, on street corners, and in popular tourist areas.

Local markets: Jordan is home to many local markets, where you can find fresh produce, spices, meats, and other ingredients. These markets are a great place to sample local foods and pick up ingredients for cooking at home. Some of the most popular markets in Jordan include the Amman Citadel Market, the Downtown Market, and the Souk Jara Market.

Traditional restaurants: Jordan has a rich culinary tradition, and there are many restaurants throughout the country that specialize in traditional Jordanian cuisine. These restaurants serve dishes such as mansaf, maqluba, and kofta, and offer an authentic dining experience in a comfortable setting.

International cuisine: In addition to traditional Jordanian cuisine, there are also many restaurants in Jordan that offer international cuisine. You can find everything from Italian and French to Asian and American cuisine in Jordan, with many restaurants featuring fusion dishes that blend local and international flavors.

Fine dining: If you're looking for a special dining experience, there are also many fine dining options in Jordan. These restaurants offer high-end cuisine, often with stunning views and elegant atmospheres. Some of the top fine dining restaurants in Jordan include Fakhr El-Din, Kan Zaman, and La Maison Verte.

Overall, Jordan offers a diverse range of dining options to suit every taste and budget. Whether you're in the mood for a quick snack on the go or a luxurious fine dining experience, you're sure to find something that satisfies your cravings in this food-loving country.

Tips for dining in Jordan

If you're planning to dine in Jordan, here are some tips to keep in mind:

Follow local customs: Jordan is a conservative country, and every visitor must respect local customs when dining out. Dress modestly and avoid public displays of affection. If you're dining during the holy month of Ramadan, be aware that many restaurants may be closed during the day.

Sample the street food: Jordan is famous for its street food, so don't be afraid to try some of the local specialties. Look for stalls that are popular with locals and make sure the food is fresh and cooked properly.

Be aware of spice levels: Jordanian cuisine can be quite spicy, so be prepared for some heat. If you're not used to spicy food, start with milder dishes and work your way up.

Try traditional dishes: Jordan has a rich culinary tradition, so be sure to try some of the traditional dishes like mansaf, maqluba, and kofta. These dishes are often served family-style and are meant to be shared.

Drink plenty of water: Jordan can get very hot and dry, so it's important to stay hydrated. Drink plenty of water and avoid tap water, which may not be safe to drink.

Tip appropriately: Tipping is not mandatory in Jordan, but it's a common practice in restaurants. A tip of 10% is usually sufficient for good service.

Be mindful of alcohol consumption: Jordan is a predominantly Muslim country, and alcohol is not widely available. If you do drink, be aware of local laws and customs and drink responsibly.

By following these tips, you'll be able to fully enjoy the dining experience in Jordan and get a taste of the country's rich culinary heritage.

Chapter 6

Culture and Customs

Jordan is a country with a rich history and diverse cultural background. From the ancient city of Petra to the modern city of Amman, Jordan offers a unique blend of old and new, traditional and modern. We will cover everything from food and music to religion and holidays. Whether you are planning a trip to Jordan or simply want to learn more about this fascinating country, this guide is for you.

Food Culture

Jordanian cuisine is a reflection of the country's diverse cultural heritage. It is influenced by Arabic, Mediterranean, and Middle Eastern culinary traditions. Some of the most popular dishes include mansaf, a traditional Jordanian dish made with lamb, yogurt, and rice, and maqluba, a layered dish of rice, vegetables, and meat.

Jordanians are known for their hospitality, and food is an important part of their culture. When invited to a Jordanian home, it is customary to bring a gift, such as sweets or flowers. Guests are often served tea or Arabic coffee and a selection of mezze, small dishes of appetizers, before the main meal.

Music and Dance

Music and dance are an important part of Jordanian culture. Traditional music is often played at weddings and other celebrations, and the dabke, a popular folk dance, is performed by both men and women.

The music of Jordan is influenced by many different cultures, including Arabic, Bedouin, and Turkish. The oud, a stringed instrument similar to a lute, is a popular instrument in Jordanian music.

Holidays and Celebrations

Jordan celebrates a number of holidays and special occasions throughout the year. Some of the most important holidays include:

Eid al-Fitr: This holiday marks the end of Ramadan, the Islamic holy month of fasting.

Eid al-Adha: This holiday commemorates the Prophet Ibrahim's willingness to sacrifice his son, as a test of faith.

Independence Day: This holiday celebrates Jordan's independence from British rule in 1946.

Christmas: Although most Jordanians are Muslims, there is a Christian community in Jordan, and Christmas is celebrated as a national holiday.

Traditional Clothing

Traditional Jordanian clothing varies depending on the region and the occasion. Bedouin women often wear colorful dresses and headscarves, while men wear a long white robe called a thobe.

In urban areas, many Jordanians wear Western-style clothing, although traditional dress is still worn on special occasions.

Art and Architecture

Jordan is home to many ancient ruins and architectural wonders, including the city of Petra. Jordanian art is influenced by Islamic and Arab traditions, and traditional crafts such as pottery, weaving, and glassblowing are still practiced.

Jordanian culture and traditions are as diverse and complex as the country itself. From the food to the music to the holidays, there is so much to explore and discover in this fascinating country. Whether you are planning a trip to Jordan or simply want to learn more about this unique culture, we hope that this guide has been informative and helpful.

Social Etiquette and Customs

In Jordan, social etiquette plays an important role in daily life. Understanding the customs and traditions of Jordan can help visitors navigate social situations with ease and show respect to the local culture. Let us explore some of the social etiquette and customs in Jordan.

Greetings and Introductions: In Jordan, it is customary to greet people with a handshake and a smile. Men typically shake hands with other men, while women may shake hands with other women or simply nod their heads in greeting. When meeting someone for the first time, it is polite to introduce oneself with a friendly greeting such as "marhaba" (hello) or "salam" (peace).

Gender Roles: Jordan is a conservative society, and traditional gender roles are still prevalent. Men are typically the primary breadwinners, while women are expected to take care of the home and family. However, this is slowly changing, and women are increasingly entering the workforce and taking on leadership roles.

Dress Code: Jordan is a Muslim country, and conservative dress is the norm. Visitors should dress modestly, covering their shoulders and knees in public. It is also respectful to remove shoes before entering someone's home or a mosque.

Hospitality: Jordanians are known for their hospitality, and guests are treated with great respect and generosity. It is customary to offer guests food and drinks, and it is considered impolite to refuse. When invited to a Jordanian home, it is also customary to bring a small gift, such as sweets or flowers.

Eating and Drinking: In Jordan, it is customary to eat with one's right hand, as the left hand is considered unclean. Visitors may also be offered a traditional Jordanian meal, such as mansaf, which is often eaten with the hands. When eating in a group, it is customary to wait for the host or hostess to begin eating before starting oneself.

Religious Customs: Jordan is a Muslim country, and visitors should be aware of certain customs and traditions related to Islam. During the holy month of Ramadan, Muslims fast from sunrise to sunset, and it is respectful for non-Muslims to refrain from eating, drinking, or smoking in public during this time. Visitors should also be aware that many businesses and restaurants may have reduced hours during Ramadan.

Language

Arabic is the official language of Jordan, but many Jordanians also speak English. Visitors who speak some Arabic may find it helpful to learn a few basic phrases, such as "shukran" (thank you) and "afwan" (you're welcome).

Understanding the social etiquette and customs in Jordan can help visitors show respect to the local culture and navigate social situations with ease. From greetings and introductions to eating and drinking, these customs are an important part of daily life in Jordan. By following these customs and traditions, visitors can experience the warmth and hospitality of Jordanian culture.

Religious Practices

Religion plays a significant role in Jordanian culture, and visitors to the country may encounter various religious practices and customs. Islam is the dominant religion in Jordan, and the majority of the population follows Sunni Islam. Here, we will explore some of the religious practices and customs in Jordan.

Prayer: Muslims are required to pray five times a day, and the call to prayer can be heard throughout the country. Visitors may notice people stopping what they are doing to pray, whether it is in a mosque or on the street. It is important to be respectful of those who are praying and avoid interrupting them.

Ramadan: This is the ninth month of the Islamic calendar, and it is considered the holiest month of the year for Muslims. During this time, Muslims fast from sunrise to sunset, and it is a time of spiritual reflection and devotion. Non-Muslims should be aware that it is respectful to refrain from eating, drinking, or smoking in public during this time.

Eid al-Fitr and Eid al-Adha: These are two important holidays in the Islamic calendar. Eid al-Fitr marks the end of Ramadan and is celebrated with feasts and gatherings with family and friends. Eid al-Adha commemorates the willingness of Prophet Ibrahim (Abraham) to sacrifice his son, and it is celebrated with the sacrifice of an animal, typically a sheep or goat.

Hijab and Dress Code: Many Muslim women in Jordan wear a headscarf known as a hijab as a symbol of modesty and faith. It is important to respect their choice to wear the hijab and to dress modestly. Visitors should avoid wearing revealing clothing in public places, and it is customary to remove shoes before entering a mosque.

Christianity and Other Religions: While Islam is the dominant religion in Jordan, Christianity and other religions are also practiced. Visitors may encounter Christian churches and other religious sites throughout the country. It is important to be respectful of these sites and the customs and traditions associated with them.

Religion is an important part of Jordanian culture, and visitors to the country may encounter various religious practices and customs. From the call to prayer to the observance of Ramadan and other important holidays, these practices are a significant part of daily life in Jordan. By being respectful and aware of these customs, visitors can explore Jordanian culture and religion.

Clothing Recommendations

As a visitor, it is important to be aware of the dress code and clothing recommendations to ensure a respectful and comfortable experience.

General Dress Code: In Jordan, dressing conservatively is recommended, especially when visiting religious sites or interacting with locals. This means avoiding revealing clothing, shorts, and sleeveless shirts. It is also recommended to dress modestly in public places, including markets and restaurants.

Head Coverings: While not mandatory for non-Muslims, it is respectful to wear a head covering when entering mosques or other religious sites. Women may wear a headscarf or shawl, while men can wear a hat or cap.

Footwear: It is customary to remove shoes before entering a mosque, a home, or any other place of worship. It is also common to remove shoes when entering someone's home. Wearing socks or stockings is recommended.

Women's Clothing: Women are recommended to dress modestly, with clothing that covers their shoulders, chest, and knees. Loose-fitting clothing is recommended, such as long skirts or dresses, loose pants, or long-sleeved tops. The hijab is not mandatory for non-Muslim women, but wearing a scarf or shawl to cover the hair is recommended when entering mosques or religious sites.

Men's Clothing: Men are recommended to dress conservatively, with long pants and shirts that cover their shoulders. T-shirts are acceptable as long as they cover the shoulders. Sleeveless shirts and shorts should be avoided in public places.

Swimwear: While swimwear is acceptable in hotels and resorts, it is recommended to wear modest swimwear that covers the chest and thighs. Bikinis and other revealing swimwear should be avoided in public places.

Jordan is a country with a rich culture and history, and respecting the dress code and clothing recommendations is an important part of experiencing this culture. By dressing modestly and being aware of the customs and traditions, visitors can ensure a respectful and comfortable experience.

Chapter 7

Outdoor Activities

If you're looking for a destination that offers a unique blend of history, culture, and adventure, then Jordan is the place for you. From hiking through ancient ruins to exploring desert landscapes, here are some of the top outdoor activities to experience in Jordan.

Hiking and Trekking

Jordan is home to some of the most spectacular hiking and trekking trails in the world. One of the most popular routes is the Jordan Trail, a 650-kilometer trek that stretches from the north to the south of the country. The trail takes hikers through a diverse range of landscapes, from the lush green hills of the north to the arid desert of the south. Along the way, hikers can experience stunning views of ancient ruins, traditional Bedouin camps, and the awe-inspiring Wadi Rum.

Another popular trek is the Dana to Petra trek, a challenging route that takes hikers through the rugged mountains and valleys of the Dana Biosphere Reserve, one of Jordan's most biodiverse areas. The trek ends at the ancient city of Petra.

Canyoning and Rock Climbing

For those who prefer a more adrenaline-fueled adventure, canyoning and rock climbing are great options in Jordan. The country is home to some of the most dramatic canyons and cliffs in the world, offering thrill-seekers a chance to test their skills and bravery.

One of the best places to go canyoning is in Wadi Mujib, a deep canyon that runs from the Dead Sea to the mountains of Moab. The canyon offers a variety of challenges, from gentle wading to abseiling down waterfalls.

Rock climbing is also a popular activity in Jordan, with many sites offering world-class routes for climbers of all levels. Some of the most popular areas include Wadi Rum, Ajloun, and the Dead Sea.

Desert Adventures

No trip to Jordan would be complete without experiencing the stunning beauty of the desert landscapes. From camel treks to hot air balloon rides, there are plenty of ways to explore the vast deserts of Jordan.

One of the most popular activities is a Jeep tour of Wadi Rum, a desert valley famous for its red sandstone formations and its connection to the famous British officer T.E. Lawrence, also known as Lawrence of Arabia. The tour takes visitors through the breathtaking landscape, stopping at famous sites such as Lawrence's Spring and the Khazali Canyon.

Another popular activity is a camel trek through the Wadi Rum desert, offering a more traditional way to experience the area. Visitors can also take a hot air balloon ride over the desert, offering a unique perspective of the landscape.

Water Sports

Jordan may be known for its deserts, but it also offers plenty of opportunities for water-based activities. The country is home to the Red Sea, one of the world's top diving destinations, as well as the Dead Sea.

Diving and snorkeling in the Red Sea are a must-do activity for any water sports enthusiast. The waters are teeming with a variety of marine life, including colorful fish, dolphins, and even the occasional whale shark. For those who prefer to stay above the water, kayaking and paddleboarding are also popular options.

The Dead Sea, on the other hand, offers a unique experience for swimmers due to its high salt concentration. The buoyancy of the water allows visitors to float effortlessly on the surface, while also offering healing properties for the skin.

Jordan offers a wealth of outdoor activities that are sure to satisfy any adventurous traveler.

Chapter 8

Shopping

One of the most popular activities for tourists is shopping, and for good reason. Jordan is a shopper's paradise, with an array of unique and high-quality goods available at great prices. Here, we will take you on a journey through the best shopping destinations in Jordan, and help you find the perfect souvenirs to take home.

Shopping Locations

Amman: The Capital City's Markets

As the capital city of Jordan, Amman is a hub for commerce and culture. The city's markets are a must-visit for any shopping enthusiast. The Downtown area of Amman is home to the famous Souk Jara, an outdoor market that sells everything from traditional clothing to handmade pottery. The market is open on Fridays from

May to September, and features live music and food vendors in addition to its shopping options.

Another popular market in Amman is the Gold Souk, located in the heart of the city. This market is the perfect place to find unique and intricate jewelry pieces, such as bracelets, necklaces, and earrings. The Gold Souk is also home to some of the best goldsmiths in the region, who can create custom pieces to your specifications.

Madaba: The City of Mosaics

Madaba is a small city located just a short drive from Amman. It is known for its stunning Byzantine-era mosaics, which can be found in churches and museums throughout the city. In addition to its cultural attractions, Madaba is also home to some excellent shopping opportunities.

One of the best places to shop in Madaba is the Haret Jdoudna market, which is located in a beautiful old house in the center of the city. The market features a variety of goods, including handmade textiles, pottery, and souvenirs. Visitors can also take a cooking class in the market's kitchen, where they will learn how to prepare traditional Jordanian dishes.

Aqaba: The Port City

Located on the Red Sea, Aqaba is a bustling port city that is popular with tourists and locals alike. The city's markets are a great place to find unique souvenirs and gifts.

The Aqaba Souk is one of the city's most popular markets, and is home to a variety of shops selling everything from spices to clothing. Visitors can also find handmade jewelry and ceramics at the market, as well as traditional Jordanian sweets.

The Souk by the Sea is another popular shopping destination in Aqaba. This market is located on the waterfront, and is the perfect place to find souvenirs and gifts to take home. Visitors can shop for handmade carpets, clothing, and jewelry, and can also sample some of the local cuisine at the market's food stalls.

Wadi Musa: The Gateway to Petra

Wadi Musa is a small town located near the ancient city of Petra. While most tourists come to the area to visit Petra, the town itself is also home to some excellent shopping opportunities.

The main market in Wadi Musa is the Al-Siq Souk, which is located just outside the entrance to Petra. This market features a variety of goods, including spices, jewelry, and textiles. Visitors can also find handmade pottery and ceramics at the market, as well as souvenirs and gifts.

Jordan is a shopper's paradise, with a variety of unique and high-quality goods available at great prices. Whether you're looking for handmade textiles, intricate jewelry, or traditional Jordanian sweets, you'll find it all in Jordan's markets.

Traditional Handicrafts

Jordan is popular for its rich cultural heritage and traditional handicrafts. Here are some popular Jordanian handicrafts that are unique and make great souvenirs:

Mosaic: Jordan is known for its beautiful mosaics that date back to the Roman era. Today, the art of mosaic making is still alive and well, with artisans creating intricate designs using tiny pieces of colored glass or ceramic tiles.

Embroidery: Jordanian embroidery is famous for its intricate designs and vibrant colors. This traditional handicraft is often used to decorate clothing, cushion covers, and other household items.

Pottery: Jordanian pottery is made using traditional techniques passed down through generations. The pottery is often decorated with intricate designs and is used for cooking, serving, and decorative purposes.

Bedouin Weaving: Bedouin weaving is a traditional Jordanian handicraft that is still practiced today. Using a traditional loom, artisans create beautiful rugs, blankets, and other textiles using wool and other natural fibers.

Copperware: Jordanian copperware is renowned for its beauty and durability. Artisans use traditional techniques to create intricate designs on pots, trays, and other household items.

Calligraphy: Arabic calligraphy is an important part of Jordanian culture, and many artisans specialize in this traditional handicraft. Using a special pen, they create beautiful designs that can be used to decorate walls, book covers, and other items.

Woodcarving: Jordanian woodcarving is another traditional handicraft that is still practiced today. Using a variety of tools, artisans create intricate designs on furniture, doors, and other wooden objects.

These are just a few examples of the many traditional handicrafts that can be found in Jordan. Each one is unique and reflects the rich cultural heritage of this fascinating country.

Shopping Tips and Recommendations

Whether you're shopping for groceries or souvenirs, here are some shopping tips and recommendations that can help you get the most out of your shopping experience:

Make a list: Before you head out to the store, make a list of the items you need. This will help you stay focused and avoid impulse purchases.

Compare prices: If you're shopping for a specific item, compare prices at different stores to find the best deal. You can also check online to see if you can find a better price.

Consider quality: While price is important, it's also important to consider the quality of the item you're buying. Sometimes it's worth paying a little extra for something that will last longer.

Don't be afraid to negotiate: In some cultures, bargaining is a common practice. If you're shopping in a market or bazaar, don't be afraid to negotiate the price of an item.

Bring your own bags: Many stores are now charging for plastic bags, so it's a good idea to bring your own reusable bags.

Check for sales: Before you start shopping, check to see if there are any sales or promotions happening at the store. You might be able to save some money on the items you need.

Be mindful of your surroundings: When you're out shopping, it's important to be aware of your surroundings. Keep an eye on your belongings and be cautious of pickpockets or other potential dangers.

By following these shopping tips and recommendations, you can make your shopping experience more efficient and enjoyable.

Chapter 9

Health and Safety

As with any travel destination, it's important to prioritize health and safety to ensure a smooth and enjoyable trip.

Here is a comprehensive guide to health and safety in Jordan, covering everything to help you plan your trip with confidence.

Water and Food Safety

Jordan's tap water is generally safe to drink in urban areas, but it's recommended to stick to bottled water, especially in more rural areas. When purchasing bottled water, make sure the seal is unbroken, and the water is from a reputable brand.

When it comes to food safety, it's generally safe to eat at established restaurants and hotels. However, be cautious when eating street food or in local markets, as the hygiene standards may not be up to par.

Sun Safety

Jordan's climate is predominantly dry and sunny, with intense heat during the summer months. It's important to take measures to protect yourself from the sun to avoid sunburn and heatstroke.

Make sure to wear sunscreen with a high SPF, a hat, and sunglasses when spending time outside. It's also a good idea to avoid spending too much time outside during the hottest parts of the day and to stay hydrated by drinking plenty of water.

Crime Rates

Jordan is considered a relatively safe country for travelers, with a low crime rate. However, as with any travel destination, it's important to take basic safety precautions.

Petty crime, such as pickpocketing and theft, can occur in crowded areas and tourist hotspots. It's important to keep your valuables secure and to be aware of your surroundings.

It's also recommended to avoid traveling alone at night, especially in more isolated areas. Women should take extra precautions when traveling alone and may want to consider dressing conservatively to avoid unwanted attention.

Medical Facilities

Jordan has a modern and well-equipped healthcare system, with public and private hospitals located throughout the country. The majority of medical staff speaks English, and the standard of care is generally good.

However, medical treatment can be expensive, especially for non-residents. It's recommended to purchase travel insurance before traveling to Jordan to ensure you're covered in case of any medical emergencies.

Natural Disasters

Jordan is located in a seismically active region and is prone to earthquakes. While earthquakes are not common, it's important to be aware of the potential risk and to take basic safety precautions in case of an earthquake.

In addition, Jordan can experience flash floods during the winter months, especially in the southern part of the country. It's important to stay informed of weather conditions and to avoid traveling to affected areas during and after heavy rainfall.

Jordan is a unique and fascinating travel destination, but it's important to prioritize health and safety when

Safety Tips

When traveling to Jordan, it's important to take basic safety precautions to ensure a smooth and enjoyable trip. Here are some tips and recommendations to keep in mind:

Be aware of your surroundings: It's always important to stay aware of your surroundings and to avoid isolated areas, especially at night.

Keep your valuables secure: Petty crime, such as pickpocketing and theft, can occur in crowded areas and tourist hotspots. Make sure to keep your valuables secure and to be aware of your surroundings.

Dress conservatively: Jordan is a conservative country, and it's important to dress appropriately, especially when visiting religious sites. Every woman should dress modestly and cover their shoulders and knees.

Stay hydrated: Jordan can get extremely hot during the summer months, and it's important to stay hydrated by drinking plenty of water.

Protect yourself from the sun: Make sure to wear sunscreen with a high SPF, a hat, and sunglasses when spending time outside.

Avoid drinking tap water: While Jordan's tap water is generally safe to drink in urban areas, it's recommended to stick to bottled water, especially in more rural areas.

Be cautious when eating street food: While Jordan has a rich culinary tradition, it's important to be cautious when eating street food or in local markets, as the hygiene standards may not be up to par.

Purchase travel insurance: Medical treatment can be expensive in Jordan, especially for non-residents. It's recommended to purchase travel insurance before traveling to ensure you're covered in case of any medical emergencies.

By following these tips and recommendations, you can help ensure a safe and enjoyable trip to Jordan.

Chapter 10

Practical Information

For those planning a trip to Jordan, it is important to understand the country's currency, money exchange options, language, and communication practices to make the most of their visit.

Currency and Money Exchange

The official currency of Jordan is the Jordanian Dinar (JOD), which is divided into 100 piasters. The dinar is a relatively strong currency, and its exchange rate is fixed to the US dollar. As of April 2023, the exchange rate is approximately 1 JOD to 1.41 USD.

Foreign currency can be exchanged at banks, exchange offices, and hotels throughout the country. However, it is important to note that exchanging money at hotels and airports can come with higher fees and lower exchange rates compared to banks and exchange offices. It is recommended to exchange money at reputable banks and exchange offices to ensure fair rates and fees.

Language and Communication

The official language of Jordan is Arabic. It is the most widely spoken language, although English is widely spoken and understood, especially in tourist areas and among younger generations. Other languages spoken in Jordan include French, German, and Spanish, among others.

Basic Arabic Phrases

If you are planning a trip to Jordan, it can be helpful to learn a few basic Arabic phrases to help you navigate the local culture and communicate with locals. While English is widely spoken in Jordan, showing an effort to communicate in Arabic can go a long way in building connections and demonstrating respect for the local culture. Here are a few basic phrases to get you started:

Greetings:

Hello: As-salamu alaykum (ah-sah-lah-moo ah-lay-koom)

Goodbye: Ma'asalama (ma-ah-sah-lah-mah)

Politeness:

Please: Min fadlak (min fahd-lahk)

Thank you: Shukran (shook-ran)

You're welcome: Afwan (ahf-wan)

Excuse me: 'An iznuk (ahn eez-nook)

Directions:

Where is...?: 'Ayna (eye-nah)...

Left: Yasar (ya-sar)

Right: Yameen (ya-meen)

Straight: Ala tool (ah-lah tool)

Food and Drink:

Water: Ma' (mah)

Tea: Shay (shy)

Coffee: Qahwa (kah-wah)

Bread: Khobz (khobz)

Vegetarian: Nabati (nah-bah-tee)

Miscellaneous:

How much?: Bish-hal? (bish-hahl)

I don't understand: Ana la afham (ah-nah lah ahf-hahm)

Do you speak English?: Hal tatakallam al-ingliziya? (hal ta-tah-kal-lam al-in-glee-zee-yah)

Learning a few basic Arabic phrases can help you connect with locals, show respect for the local culture, and make your travels in Jordan more enjoyable and rewarding.

In addition, it is important to note that communication in Jordan can be indirect and nuanced, with an emphasis on politeness and respect. It is common to exchange pleasantries and engage in small talk before getting down to business. Non-verbal communication, such as gestures and facial expressions, can also play a significant role in communication in Jordan.

Money Exchange Tips

When exchanging money in Jordan, it is important to be aware of common scams and tricks that can be used to take advantage of unsuspecting travelers. One common scam involves offering a higher exchange rate for larger bills, but then counting the bills incorrectly or switching them out for counterfeit bills. To avoid falling victim to these scams, it is best to only exchange money at reputable banks and exchange offices, and to count your money carefully before leaving.

Another important consideration when exchanging money in Jordan is to have a variety of smaller bills and coins on hand, as many smaller businesses and markets may not have the ability to break large bills.

Jordan is a beautiful and diverse country with much to offer visitors. By understanding the country's currency and money exchange options, as well as its language and communication practices, travelers can make the most of their visit and avoid common pitfalls.

Conclusion

After exploring the vibrant country of Jordan through this travel guide, it can be concluded that Jordan is a place to be for any traveler seeking an immersive and culturally rich experience.

From the ancient city of Petra to the natural wonder of the Dead Sea, Jordan offers a diverse range of attractions that cater to all types of travelers.

Moreover, Jordan is a safe and hospitable country that welcomes visitors with open arms. Its people are friendly and always willing to help, ensuring that travelers have a comfortable and enjoyable stay.

Overall, a trip to Jordan is a unique and unforgettable experience that will leave travelers with a deeper appreciation for the region's history, culture, and natural beauty. Our travel guide provides all the necessary information for planning a successful and memorable trip to Jordan, making it an essential resource for any traveler embarking on a journey to this enchanting destination.

Printed in Great Britain
by Amazon

26265975R00069

Jordan is a safe and hospitable country that welcomes visitors with open arms. Its people are friendly and always willing to help, ensuring that travelers have a comfortable and enjoyable stay.

Overall, a trip to Jordan is a unique and unforgettable experience that will leave travelers with a deeper appreciation for the region's history, culture, and natural beauty.

Our travel guide provides all the necessary information for planning a successful and memorable trip to Jordan, making it an essential resource for any traveler embarking on a journey to this enchanting destination.

ISBN 9798391454526

90000